Read-About® Geography

Minnesota

By Sean Dolan

Consultants
Reading Adviser
Nanci R. Vargus, EdD
Assistant Professor of Literacy
University of Indianapolis, Indianapolis, Indiana

Subject Adviser
Enid Costley, MLS
Children's Librarian
Hibbing Public Library
Hibbing, Minnesota

Children's Press®
A Division of Scholastic Inc.
New York   Toronto   London   Auckland   Sydney
Mexico City   New Delhi   Hong Kong
Danbury, Connecticut

Designer: Herman Adler Design
Photo Researcher: Caroline Anderson
The photo on the cover shows Minneapolis, Minnesota.

Library of Congress Cataloging-in-Publication Data

Dolan, Sean.
  Minnesota / by Sean Dolan.
    p. cm. — (Rookie read-about geography)
  Includes index.
  ISBN 0-516-25257-7 (lib. bdg.)   0-516-25158-9 (pbk.)
  1. Minnesota—Juvenile literature. 2. Minnesota—Geography—Juvenile
literature. I. Title. II. Series.
  F606.3.D65 2005
  917.76'02—dc22   2005002089

CHILDREN'S PRESS, and ROOKIE READ-ABOUT®,
and associated logos are trademarks and/or registered trademarks
of Scholastic Library Publishing. SCHOLASTIC and associated logos
are trademarks and/or registered trademarks of Scholastic Inc.

1 2 3 4 5 6 7 8 9 10 R 14 13 12 11 10 09 08 07 06 05

Which state is known as the Land of 10,000 Lakes?

It's Minnesota!

Minnesota has many lakes.
Only four counties in
Minnesota do not have
a lake.

Minnesota is in the north
central part of the United
States. Can you find it on
this map?

CANADA

WASHINGTON
OREGON
IDAHO
MONTANA
NORTH DAKOTA
SOUTH DAKOTA
WYOMING
NEBRASKA
IOWA
MINNESOTA
WISCONSIN
MICHIGAN
NEW HAMPSHIRE
VERMONT
MAINE
NEW YORK
MASSACHUSETTS
RHODE ISLAND
CONNECTICUT
NEW JERSEY
DELAWARE
MARYLAND
PENNSYLVANIA
Washington, D.C.
NEVADA
UTAH
CALIFORNIA
COLORADO
KANSAS
MISSOURI
ILLINOIS
INDIANA
OHIO
WEST VIRGINIA
VIRGINIA
KENTUCKY
ARIZONA
NEW MEXICO
OKLAHOMA
ARKANSAS
TENNESSEE
NORTH CAROLINA
SOUTH CAROLINA
TEXAS
MISSISSIPPI
ALABAMA
GEORGIA
LOUISIANA
FLORIDA

North
West   East
South

ALASKA
CANADA
MEXICO
HAWAII

Split Rock Lighthouse is on the shore of Lake Superior.

Minnesota has forests,
plains, lakes, and rivers.

The largest lake in
the United States is on
Minnesota's border. It
is called Lake Superior.
It is one of the five
Great Lakes.

The second-longest river in the United States begins in Minnesota. It is called the Mississippi River. It begins at Lake Itasca.

These people are canoeing on the Mississippi River.

10

Northern Minnesota is the rockiest part of the state. It has cliffs, deep lakes, and thick forests.

Minnesota's trees and lakes make perfect nesting places for birds. The state bird is the common loon.

This is a white-tailed deer.

Minnesota's forests are home to larger animals, too. There are white-tailed deer, black bears, red foxes, and timber wolves.

This is a timber wolf.

The Mesabi Range, in north central Minnesota, is the largest producer of iron ore in the United States.

Mining is still important in Minnesota.

Most farms in Minnesota are in the flat, southern part of the state. Farmers grow wheat, corn, hay, and soybeans.

This is a soybean farm.

Minnesota also has dairy farms. These farms produce milk, cheese, and butter.

Minneapolis is the largest city in Minnesota. St. Paul, which is across the river from Minneapolis, is the state capital.

Together, Minneapolis and St. Paul are known as the Twin Cities.

CANADA

NORTH DAKOTA

MINNESOTA

Mississippi River

SOUTH DAKOTA

WISCONSIN

Minneapolis ● ☆ St. Paul

North
West ✦ East
South

SCALE 1 inch = 90 miles

0   Miles   90

0   Kilometers   145

IOWA

Near Minneapolis and St. Paul is the city of Bloomington. You can visit the Mall of America there.

You can shop in more than 500 stores and ride a roller coaster in this mall.

Minnesota has long, cold winters. Parts of Minnesota can be covered in snow from November to April.

Summers are warm in Minnesota. People like to go camping, boating, and fishing.

What would you like to do in Minnesota?

Words You Know

camping

cliff

common loon

dairy farm

Index

About the Author

Sean Dolan is a writer, songwriter, and musician. He has written more than thirty books for young readers.

Photo Credits

Photographs © 2005: Corbis Images: 17, 31 top right (James L. Amos), 10, 19, 30 top left, 30 bottom right (Layne Kennedy); Dembinsky Photo Assoc./Richard Hamilton Smith: 26, 30 top right; Greg Ryan/Sally Beyer: 3, 9, 18, 25, 31 bottom left; Index Stock Imagery/William Ervin: 15, 31 bottom right; National Geographic Image Collection/Michael S. Quinton: 13, 30 bottom left; PhotoEdit/James Shaffer: 22; Stone/Getty Images/Daniel J. Cox: 14; Taxi/Getty Images/Gary Randall: cover; The Image Works: 29 (Sjkold) 6, 31 top left (Joe Sohm).
Maps on pages 5, 21 by Bob Italiano

Lake Superior

mining

Mississippi River

timber wolf

31